CRUSHED WILD MINT

CRUSHED WILD MINT

JESS HOUSTY

NIGHTWOOD EDITIONS

2023

Nightwood Editions
P.O. Box 1779
Gibsons, BC VON 1V0
Canada
www.nightwoodeditions.com

COVER DESIGN: Angela Yen
TYPOGRAPHY: Libris Simas Ferraz / Onça Design

Nightwood Editions acknowledges the support of the Canada Council for the Arts, the Government of Canada, and the Province of British Columbia through the BC Arts Council.

This book has been produced on 100% post-consumer recycled, ancient-forest-free paper, processed chlorine-free and printed with vegetable-based dyes.

Printed and bound in Canada.

LIBRARY AND ARCHIVES CANADA CATALOGUING IN PUBLICATION

Title: Crushed wild mint / Jess Housty.
Names: Housty, Jess, author.
Identifiers: Canadiana (print) 20230444253 | Canadiana (ebook) 20230444261 |
    ISBN 9780889714502 (softcover) | ISBN 9780889714519 (EPUB)
Subjects: LCGFT: Poetry.
Classification: LCC PS8615.O88 C78 2023 | DDC C811/.6—dc23

For my father and all the poems he wrote in Ellerslie.

CONTENTS

V

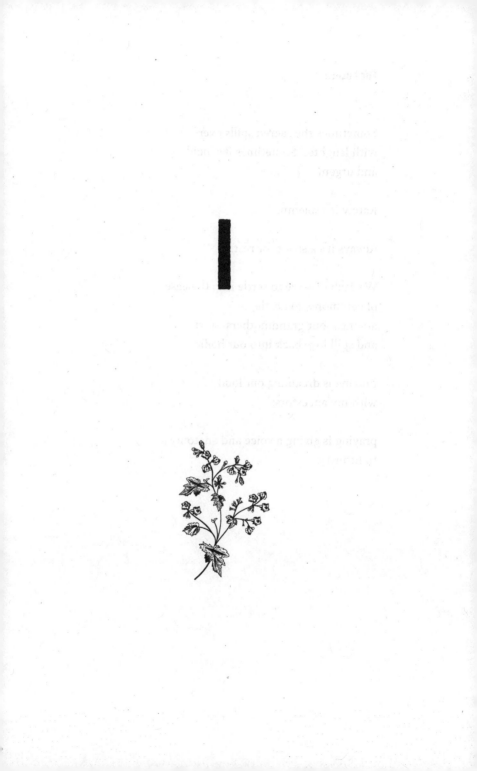

The Future

Sometimes the sacred spills over
with laughter. Sometimes it's lucid
and urgent.

Rarely it's solemn.

Always it's a space for rest.

We each deserve to settle into the ease
of ceremony, to nestle
amongst our grandmothers' skirts
and spill love back into our bodies.

Praying is dreaming out loud
with my ancestors;

praying is giving a voice and anatomy
to futurity.

Nearshore Prayer

This is a prayer that extends
in the direction of the ocean:

it is not a story; nothing
is apocryphal in prayer.

(You taught me that water
is the most practised lapidary—
that it can shape and polish
all precious things, not just stone:
heart and breath, bone
and grief.

Through you I know
that water has mastered us.)

Ocean, as I step into you
I ask that you seek out what is precious
in me; etch it with your salt fingers
and smooth it against the dip and rise
of your sleeping chest.

Make me curious about what is absent.
Let me redefine wholeness
by what is left behind when your hands
are lifted away from my body,
when you've taken what is no longer
mine to carry.

Weather Diptych

Where is your windy heart
when the trees dip and shake
like old chiefs
nodding eagle down
onto the floor?

Is it lifting upward,
toward the clouds?
Or is it leaning low and close
to the ground below you?

What part of your heart
is made of feathers?
What part of stone?

(We are unsure
whether we're incapable of flight
or the sky is too tired
to carry us.)

    * * *

Where is your rainy heart
when the day is still
as an old woman's hands
resting in her lap
during ceremony?

Is it quiet and trembling
like a breath held too long?
Or is it loud as a rattle
and bright as ochre?

What part of your heart
is made of feathers?
What part of stone?

(We are unsure
whether we float
or the water
uplifts us.)

Ruminant / Remnant

Take in the kindness of your medicine
like a deer does: chew it slowly,
then slowly again. Grind your gentle mouthful
of wild rose petals, your field mint,
the sweet, deep sting of your nettles.

Or is the season late? Let the slight bitterness
of living things awaiting winter limn your tongue
with unskilled electric green. Let the soft rot
of crab apples in November disintegrate
into the spaces between your teeth
where untold stories wait.

These things will blossom again in the night
of your tender belly; reawaken to their power
as you rest the medicines inside you, layer
by layer: now yarrow, now crisp and bright plantain,
now alder bark with its sharp tannins, and so on
until you have laid something down for every story
you'll let me quietly lift out from the birdsong sorrow
you hold in your mouth.

None of this medicine is wasted; it remains, immutable,
inside of you. If I were to gut you like a deer,
the smell of good earth and the clarity of green things,
the musk and the humus, that scent would rise up
like a prayer to an ancestor so nearby
that perhaps you are still grieving them.

If I cracked open your bones, what would I find
thriving in the loam of your marrow? If you received
that final healing of ancestral becoming, what
        medicines
would be nourished by the body you'd leave behind?

Of course, my shining girl, you are not a deer,
and it is not time for you to reciprocate the medicines
by feeding what will heal babies not yet born.
Each part of you is precious, and even if delicate,
also yew-like in its resilience. In this moment,
there is no space for impossibilities like brokenness
or decay.

There is only a pocket full of licorice fern,
sea asparagus to pluck at your inner cheeks with its
        salt,
and the sweetness of wild berries for you to chew
        slowly
and chew again.

Bowing to Yarrow (I)

Who prayed out loud to the ancestors
of this yarrow? Was it your grandmother,
or her grandmother?

They prayed over the licorice fern,
the yew and the blisters of conifer sap;
they prayed over the cedar;
and now the descendants of those plant kin
carry those prayers forward to you.

This is the directionality of prayer—
it is moving all around us and through time.

As you bend to your harvests,
pray to the future and ask the yarrow
to embody those prayers, to pass them down
the family lines to your grandchildren's
grandchildren.

This is how we bind our medicine
in the world.

Mirror-Touch Synesthesia

When you gut an animal
I feel the pressure on my clavicle,
knife tugged down to soft belly
through the faint resistance of muscle.

I know the arc of the motion
and the tension in your wrist
as your bare hands sweep through viscera;
I know the tenderness of your efficiency.

This is not moralizing:
your strong fingers are factual, prime,
and I feel them.

When you gut an animal
I feel my hot blood relieved
by cool October air, feel the lightening
and lightening and lightening of selfhood
unburdened by blood and entrails.

There is no waste here, reducing
chaotic wholeness to simple nourishment,
and I feel it; I am simplified.

I feel it until I feel nothing,
vision darkening for a moment
until my body calls my own spirit back
and your hands bless the creature
that is not me, not us, but blesses us
and nourishes us.

You Are Inseparable

Carry it with you.

The dirt of your motherland unapologetic
beneath your nails,

the splinters and thorns
that work medicine under your skin:

this is the land striving to give you
a sovereign ground within your body.

You are a whole territory,
containing king tides and contour lines
and scars that curl like moss,
like rivers.

Your body is a government.
Carry it with you.

There are flocks of songbirds
sleeping in your hair,
deer's wisdom compacted in your heels,
salmon in the creeks of your veins.

Your body and the land
have collaborated for your safety and joy
and for your weightless autonomy,

and it's your sacred responsibility
to thrive within the mutual laws
they've written.

6.6.22

What causes the wound
and what heals it?

How can we treat
both things with
gentleness?

Bowing to Yarrow (II)

Imagine the words that plants are praying back to us,
repeating the intergenerational prayers of grannies
who tended these medicine patches—
translated into the nimble language of botany.

The healing of your body through sap and thistle,
root and leaf is wrought by plant and human
      matriarchs
who spoke sacredness into being together,
trusting our descendant hands to tend
these descendant medicines
and mutually renew their prayerful conversation
through our small acts of healing and propagation—
through shared, magical utterance.

Speak to your medicines, sweet ones,
so our grandchildren will someday thrive
through the prayers we negotiated
with the flora who are our kin;
speak to your medicines and learn to pray
in stem and shoot, stalk and root, berry
and balm for your someday-grandchildren's hearts.

What will you ask the medicines to embody?

Máɬuala

Who taught you how to pray?

Was it someone who loved you,
whose love made your spirit
and your body cohere?

Less palm to palm
and more palm to water,
sole to shore, brow to sun,
brow to rain.

Who taught you how to pray?

Did they feel tenderness
when they showed you,
or were they trying to unmake you?

Prayer is never fragmentary,
child; it is joints and tendons;
it binds us; it is never the knife.

Breath

Take a fistful of wild rose petals.

Be unhurried as you pile them
on your outstretched tongue
and feel their surprising weight;

grind their full perfume in your molars
and turn your breath into medicine.

It's your right to be in pain, my love.

One of my children believes
that all wind originates
in the bellies of wolves,
that storms come from their howling.

What if we howled roses?

Maybe we could trust
that the rains to come would be soft.

It's also your right to heal.

ƛásákv

In the absence of god,
bless people anyway.

We are all islands
that are joined beneath the sea
and in the absence of a sea
we are a continent.

Blessings are the way
we impart a sense of belonging;

bless others liberally
and hold your own palms
wide and empty
as a waiting sea.

A Loon, Alone

A loon,
alone,
is the idea
of a
ghost.

Two loons
are a ghost
talking
to itself
in haunting
mutterings,

in rattling
exclamations
of loneliness.

No one
has proven
that three loons
exist.

A loon,
alone,
is the memory
of a ghost.

Luật

i.

These are the poems I write
in my grandmother's kitchen:

Set out four cups of tea—
one for each of us,
one for the guest
who may soon, we hope,
cross the threshold,
and one for the ghosts
who feel safe here.

Everyone is nourished in this place.

ii.

These are the poems I write
in my grandmother's bedroom:

What's on the walls
or between the walls
is of no real consequence to us.

What makes this space safe
is love, who, with scarred and swollen knuckles,
turns away hardness at the door
and gently closes it
behind us again.

iii.

These are the poems I write
in my grandmother's living room:
You must always know
who needs a place to rest.

You must always know
who might be hungry.

iv.

These are the poems I write
in my grandmother's attic:

Every exhale expended in this house
is stacked in here, this wooden lung,
this library of breath—

snorts of anger scoring the wood erratically
as though sharp-cornered boxes
and blunt furniture
were tossed in here,
sighs of pleasure
smoothing the grain to a high gleam,
the whole place polished
by held breaths belatedly let go.

v.

These are the poems I write
in my grandmother's garden:

Which one is the prayer?

The crocus, the lily
or the tenacious weed?

Which one is the answer?

The crimson rhubarb casting
broad shadows?

The feral blackberry
pushing up from underneath
the gate?

vi.

These are the poems I write
in my grandmother's absence:
Your house is full of little altars,
your dresser, your windowsill.

But you are the prayer, the flower.

You are the love.

You are the guest we will wait for
until we're ghosts;
you are the ghost we nourish.

Where does mercy exist?

When the power cuts out, you can hear
the snow fall. We ask who needs stew, sweet tea,
a load of firewood or a little gasoline.

People bend against the Arctic outflows
to love one another.

We are all speaking quietly
as though to avoid waking others,
but the truth is all of us are wide-eyed
in the darkness, seeking each other out
for comfort.

The hum comes from all around me now:
some of us are speaking to our neighbours,
some to our lovers, some to our children
and some to our ancestors,
but we all talk low and slow
to make the night into a ritual of connection.

This is how we utter ceremony,
and ceremony builds bridges across the darkness—
a blanket gifted or loaned, an armful of kindling,
a prayer.

Ǧáǧṃ (i)

When you were tired,
we loosened our braids
and took down our hair
so our full power could arrest Death
and you could invite him
to walk with you.

And when you left us
we shook out our wild hair,
combed it with our fingers,
and braided the world
back into order for a moment.

We accepted that you
had birthed and raised
four generations of the medicine
you would need in life,

that in your absence
we have to become
our own medicine now.

So we cut our hair almost to the root
and said goodbye to Death
and lifted our faces to the sun and the rain
and invited our power to grow again
in the rich soil of our grief.

12.15.21
For bell hooks

If love is an action
(and it is),
becoming an ancestor
must be an act of perpetual love;

let our loving be a discipline

and let us feel comfort
that we can pray to you now.

Aunties

i.

We are here to speak with love
of what is overlooked.

We are here to speak with tenderness
of what is overladen.

We are here to hold our palms
at the base of a cluster of fiddleheads
and say, "Your tight spirals
are beautiful, sisters,
but so is the trust with which you unfurl."

Let us be the roots.

Let us be the light.

Let us be what stretches, broad
and vital, in between.

ii.

Who is at your back?

I bring my ancestors
in all their humanity;
you bring yours.

While we dislodge our grief
with sacred laughter,
lean into one another
like the river to the bank,

are our ancestors laughing too?

Are our great-grannies and aunties
and mothers who have gone on ahead
sitting side by side in the sunshine,
at the river,

holding and upholding each other
the same way you are present for me?

iii.

You invite me to feed
my softness.

You invite me to
revolutionary rest.

Your own softness
makes this permissible—

the sweetness and grace
of your emergence
from respite, transformed.

I wanted to hold myself
in the shape of your strength
but you call me to recognize
the strength I did not see
in myself:

the gentleness of a seed
relaxing into good soil,
the power of a root
asking for nourishment
without apology.

iv.

As I stand up and speak
to my good work in this life,
I will continue to gesture
to the space where you once stood
beside me;

this is to acknowledge
the strength you have given me.

When I speak to what gives me
power, my answer will include
a blessing of your ancestors
for bringing your abundant gifts

into this world that we share.

Sixty-Eight Plums

When sixty-eight golden plums
appear like a bowl of phosphorescence
on your stoop, look both upward
and all around you
when you give a little thanks.

It is no small feat
that they have arrived here:

Someone planted trees,
smiling to themselves at the foolishness
of growing plums in this climate
where the rain makes everything soft—
makes everyone soft.

And for more than one hundred years
the trees have probably not been tended
but certainly been spared the axe
and the lightning and unhappy accidents,
and survived to delight you.

And this week, this week of softening
and relentless rain, someone lifted their hand
level with their heart or higher—
sixty-eight times to the branches
while shaking the weather
out of their hair—
and doing this, they thought of you.

So plunge your clean hands in the bowl
(What else is there to do?)
and pick out the stems and leaves;
tear into the rain-soft flesh,
the sun-bright flesh, to pry out the pits;
and think of how you will carry forward joy
when you leave jars of warm jam
on many doorsteps in the morning.

Ǧáǧm̓ (II)

To learn the language, you said,
I should first eat a mouthful of soil from the
    motherland
each day, then pray aloud the words I tasted.

This is how I became fluent in warblers' songs,
in deluge, in the whispers of moss.
This is how I learned to listen and to pray.

But the land began to stutter
when the dull blade of your breath
dragged across the thinning light and severed it;
it yawned to make room for your small body,
your still body, and then it stopped speaking to me
while we grieved you together.

Now the soil on my tongue gives me minerals
but no stories, and without you,
I need to learn to pray without language—
to pray without ceasing—to pray like moss, or a bird.

Skuusiid

I prayed to Wúgvmi for the gift of uncles,
for humble and generous protectors,
but I didn't expect them to manifest
on city sidewalks—

to appear with kind eyes and laughter,
no ravens in earshot, rich teachings
audible even over urban chatter.

Treaties build a rib cage
around the steady heart of governance
but our sovereignty is personal and interpersonal,
upheld by small acts of love
and fingers that point
to the constellations by which such love
navigates.

City uncles are necessary magic:
direction when we are distant
from the landmarks of our homelands,
kindness when kindness is surprising,

architects of unasked for abundance.

You were a bringer of uneasy gifts,
having lived past awe into old age:
an eagle, sombre, tailfeathers battered,
a sky-being colliding with the ocean
like the remains of a star.

The tenderness you required
restored all dignity when we drew you
from the ocean. You came out gently,
rested eerily still in our arms;
you accepted warmth and invited empathy
as we dried your salty wings
and fed you a final meal.

The children hoped, as only children can hope,
that in the morning you'd be ready
to seek your next updraft. But we had
our premonitions: death was close to you.

Why else would you come to rest in the sea,
you brilliant and weary clan animal,
on what would have been my grandfather's
hundredth birthday? Why else would you come
to us?

It was not without sadness that we found you
laid out this morning, ragged and regal.
It was not without disquietude
that I stepped into the chill and clarity
of a blue February day, cradling you like a child.
And it was not without forgivable guilt
that I whispered my blessings to you,
peeled back your ethereal down like moss from a log,
methodically stripped your wings of their flight
        feathers.

In the end, only restless peace was left to me,
and only rest left to you.

Your small feathers are scattered to the wind now—
your deplumed body given back to the earth—
and in the hushed moments of the day,
I find bits of down in my hair, on my clothing,
even on my tongue. You are ceremony already.

You were a bringer of uneasy gifts,
but you asked for trust and tenderness
and who are we to turn away from your salt wings,
your shuddering toward warmth,
the abundance of your unutterable
blessings?

To the scientist who called my beloved salmonberries "insipid"

Your terse description
in some field guide I discovered as a teen
disrupted my love for those berries;

finding pleasure in them felt shameful.

I thought you must know something
I was too naive to realize—that you
were somehow more intimate with them
than I could be.

I admit I gave the whims of scientists
too much weight. No more.

I picked those berries for my granny
as a child—heaping, healing bowls
that she'd divide between us

until I read your dictum
and began to feel they must be unworthy.

I reclaim them now, and I ask their forgiveness:
they are my kin and they are rich.

I'm sorry they don't bless your table.
Everyone deserves salmonberries.

In her old age, I made my granny
sticky jelly from the fruits.
She ate it with the pleasure of a child
as she leaned against the heavy wall
of her dementia; in the end,
she wouldn't eat her toast
without a thick, sweet layer.

She's seven months gone now
and as those pink blossoms appear
joyfully, ahead of all other flowers in this place,
it is sobering to know
she won't be here to share my overflowing berry bowls
      this spring.

I'm glad I let go of your abrupt ingratitude and bad
      opinions
in time to give her the gift of salmonberry jelly;
she thought I invented it
but really, it invented our bliss.

I hope I carry her delight
as my truth and taxonomy
until I'm an elder who also has no time
for fault-finding about our berry kin.

Gwani Taught Me

That every berry in my basket
is one syllable of a prayer.

That long prayers are nourishing
but so are short ones;
the important thing is to always pray.

That the ways our bodies are nurtured
and our fingertips stained
are how we internalize sacredness.

That the motions of reaching,
of bending, of delicately picking,
are how we externalize love.

Ǧáǧíⁿ (III)

Turn around.
Look behind you.

What is it
that gives you life?

What is it
that gives life
to what gives you life?

* * *

When the Elder
brushed me with cedar
and invited me
to call on the Creator,

I was unsurprised
that Her face appeared to me
as my grandmother's face.

Transformation

There are mornings
when I feel a non-specific
loneliness
sitting soft and heavy in my bones,

hushing my surroundings
with the weight of estuary silt
and the stillness of salt.

I'd prefer the companionship
of my other forms, my animal selves,
the ones I could speak into being
if I was nimble as an ancestor.

I can't call that power down—
nor can I sit
with the silence
of my only self.

I imagine the stubble
of pinfeathers,
the different arc
of my bones
if they bent to the posture
of a carnivore.

I grieve for the lost bodies,
the self
that is singular,
that can never become the community
one ancestor might have embodied—

that can never transform.

But then there is my grandmother,
with her strong hands
and their sedge-root veins—
hands that have skinned hundreds,
thousands of ducks
in her lifetime—

When she sends me those ducks now to prepare,
with patience and a little grace from the birds
my hands no longer cramp
as I slip the skin and feathers
away from the meat;

the steam from their guts
in the cool air
makes it easy to imagine
the truth
of how my ancestors transformed—

less an act of becoming
and more an act of believing,
slipping out of our
selves
and into ourselves—

an act
sharp and sweet
as the smell of blood
and half-digested grass.

I understand
that the heart is where you hold your power
and the hands are where you hold your
sacredness,
and with wild meat on your tongue
you might even remember
the animals you become in your dreams.

And the tangle of veins in my hands that slip
between the fat and the meat,
between the copper and the sweetness,
must match the tangle of roots
in an estuary somewhere.

If I carry a likeness
of some small part of the homeland
in my body,
then I hold the possibility
that the imprint of each wolf
or bird
or small, careful creature
that walks across it
may be written on my heart.

And that is enough.

Stone

i.

Salmon scales, damselflies,
the tailfeathers of a hummingbird—
brittle barnacles, a mink's teeth,
soft river silt—
some of the blood is mine.

Moss, scrub cedar, a deer's jaw
bleached by pale sunlight—
Creek foam, dark soil,
sparrow bones—
some of the blood is mine, love.
Starlight, starfish, starflower,
stone—

some of it is mine.

ii.

And I will move in centuries
over your body, in millennia, carving you
with my two bare hands like glaciers,
marking you slowly with my teeth
and my fingernails to build fish traps
and rock art and sweet middens
across the landscape of your body.

And I will build villages in the crook
of your arm, and teach salmon to swim
in your veins of bright water,
and I will live and die in the deep inlets
of your soft body
with your hair like kelp,
with your hair like spruce roots,
wrapped around us both as we sigh
into the rain and the slow bleed.

Some of the blood is mine, love,
none of it is yours, some is the sky's
and it will paint the brief story of our love
into the stone from which stories and blood
will someday be washed away,

washed into the sea like the bones of people
and the bones of birds.

iii.

Night slept on, and the shadow ocean
was like the taut, stretched breast
of a skinned jay,
like the inner surface of a mussel shell
when the meat is stripped away.

You sank your teeth in, love, my love,
and some of the blood was mine
and some was the ocean's
and none of it was yours.

iv.

Some of the blood was mine, love,
and none of it was yours, and some of it belonged
to the little wrens with their fragile beaks
and their precious claws that harmed nothing
in this frail world.

Banquet

Sweet raven cracking me open
like a clamshell dropped from the sky:

I will make your feathers shine.

Bright raven nudging me apart
with your beak:

I will be your updraft, your rest.

Hungry raven savouring me:

I will fill your hollow bones
with prayer.

Soft raven, I am your perpetual
and living feast; I will wait for you;
I bring the light.

H̓ḷxvbís

i.

You came to me bleeding
and you held your pain close like some delicate thing,
like a fistful of owl feathers,
like the sweet proof of grief.

I gathered up driftwood worked through by
     shipworms
to teach your veins and arteries a new map for your
     blood;
I covered your body with sap from a spruce tree, my
     love;
I handed you bulrushes and the shafts of feathers.

But your blood was a story that flowed in the telling,
and you told it to me steady and bright,
and you settled the words onto my shoulders
as steady as an owl alighting on a low branch,
as sweet and irrefutable as grief,
as brittle as grief.

You said it was so,
my love, and it was so.

ii.

You came to me aching
in an agony of light, and the luminescence
of your cedar-creek skin
drew the light in me toward you
as you trembled against the outer dark.

You can gather up the light, my love, like water;
you can suffer and you can nourish
and you can let it run cool through your hair
and between your shoulder blades.

You can speak the light like a story about water
and nourish us both with the telling.

You said it was so,
my love, and it was so.

iii.

You came to me burning
and for every word you ever concealed beneath your
     bird's-tongue,
my love, the sky carved a shape between your
     shoulders
with fire, and light, and the elegance of the swallow.

Each stolen word spoke itself aloud, then,
and together they told the story of your betrayals
and your winter hardness,
the hunger that sank its teeth into your flesh
at the signal of the first snow.

Some birds migrate and some transform
when the chill shakes their feathers and the promise of
     day is short.

You said it was so,
my love, and it was so.

iv.

You came to me limping
with a casual note of sadness in your voice,
sadness mimicked by each vertebra that radiated out,
repeated like a softly spoken story,
into each one of your bones.

I will wait a long time to see what you've written
in the irregular loops and edges of your marrow;
until the ravens have laughed
with their beaks against your rib cage,
until all the little insects have whispered out their
        hunger
and burrowed warm under your scapulae,
I will listen to you patiently
as you tell me every story but the true one that waits
behind a multitude of wings.

You said it was so,
my love, and it was so.

v.

You came to me weeping
but the sweet saltwater made your eyes bright like a
    wet fern,
and the lines it pulled softly through the loam of your
    cheeks
were like slow breaths taken before song.

Your grief unfurled like a little green fern,
cautious and inevitable, delicate and undeniable,
and the earth of your skin was not a story
but a bounty and a richness
from which stories are born.

You said it was so,
my love, and it was so.

Shore

I'm sorry for the times you needed me
and I was with the shorebirds,
oblivious to the intricacies of your sorrow.

What you grieved was not lesser
than fog or eelgrass—not simpler
than shorelines that shift with the tides.

I didn't mean to choose the ocean.
There were always flat stones by me
for you and your sadness to sit on.

This is the place where sorrow is
transubstantiated; this is the place.
No one is unwelcome here.

I'm sorry for the times you needed me
and I was at the shoreline, waiting.
But bring your sorrow sweetly to me now.

Anatomy

i.

Open up your hands:
will I see lines on your palms
like cracks in dry earth,
or the imprint of curved talons?
The remembrance of high perches
and small, warm-blooded animals?

ii.

Open up your throat:
you are subtle, my love,
my lutescent warbler,
but your song I would know
even in this cacophony—
this chorus of wild, joyous
passerines.

iii.

Open up your belly:
will I see round, smooth seeds
or whiplike brittle stars?
A puff of air and feathers
or just a hint of meadow grass?
I think you do not know.
I think we will discover together
what it is that nourishes you.

iv.

Open up your chest:
will I find words buried
behind your ribs
like a midden,
like a riverbank?
Will I find words like stones,
like gleaming shells
in heavy earth?

Wilderness

I will love you into the grave
(yours or mine).

I say this not to be ghoulish
but with the simple authority of crushed mint
or migratory birds arriving and departing.

This is dependent on nothing.
It is without conditions.

I will love you into the grave
(yours or mine).

If yours, I will plant wild roses at your feet
and tell stories to the sweet insects
that chatter against your bones beneath the black
     earth;
I will make them reckon with your goodness
and we will tally up together the enormity of your
     loving.

I will love you into the grave
(yours or mine).

If mine, I will go to it quietly like an animal to the
        wakeless forest
when its time is come; I will have nothing left to ask
        for;
I will have come home and home again every day of
        my life
to rest in the wilderness of your love.

Beneath My Hands

i.

What can you recognize by touch?

Can you feel out bog cranberries
in the sphagnum, different species of clams
by the ridges of their shells?

Can you identify your lover
by the feeling of the back of their neck
beneath your hand?

ii.

What belongs to my left hand,
non-dominant?
Your right hip; a trailing line of salal bushes
as I walk; last night's spiderwebs,
dewy, against my fingertip;
all that I want but do not need.

And what belongs to my right,
where desire and necessity merge into urgency?

The broad sweep of your torso;
clear water pooled in my palm
when I'm thirsty; a fistful of broad-leaved plantain
to heal my wounds.

iii.

Beneath my hands you are the sweetness of light;
you satisfy thirst.

You have the clarity of bright weather.
You are wild fruit and wild salt;

you are healer and nourisher and edible prayer.

Cormorant

To the lone cormorant
that sits on the black buoy
at the entrance to the harbour:

I'm sorry for each time
I sent you belly first
into the water, inelegant,
scuttling toward being airborne.

Let's both acknowledge
there's so much we'll never know
about one another—

I have no idea what a sculpin
tastes like (salty?) or how it feels
(beatific?) to stretch two wings
to dry in the wind.

If you knew the love
waiting for me on the dock
I think you wouldn't begrudge
the sharp turn of my boat
that propels you from your perch.

But think of what we have
in common: both of us holding
in that liminal space
between departure and arrival,

then both of us surging forward,
clumsy, heartbeats accelerating.

For a brief moment, we are like sisters
in the mutual chaos
of flight and possibility.

Wild Crab Apples

Your breasts are wrens
abalone shells

Your breasts are arcs of rain

Your nipples are wild crab apple pits
worked smooth by an unhurried tongue

Your body is a river

You are a feast of fog, a bed of moss
and feathers

You are a songbird's flightpath
a crush of green sedge, a supplication

an abundance

The more I am nourished
the more you are replenished

and I believe this, here
is the holiest kind of loving

IV

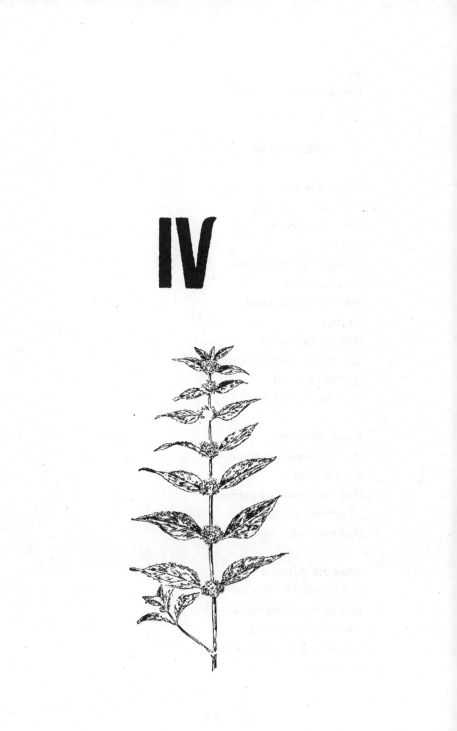

Wá

For Cecil Paul

    i. Who are you?

Some of us are struggling
   to iterate the void.
Some have felt its edges
and learned
to gently break the caul,
believing then
that they've invented
rivers,
though the rivers
have always been with us
to bind our grief,
to make us good.

Some of us know
that our bones are stones
in a riverbed,
that our bodies are defined
by embankments
that sway with our breath.

Some are softened
and rounded by this knowing,
leaning into what erodes us
until our every atom
is a reflection in the gleaming
of the water.

ii. Who are you really?

There is hurt in this world;
only a river can make it right.

If you carry the hard shape
of unknowing
snagged between your collarbones,
the river will flow around it
and the water will lift it away.

You might think a river
deals only in intangibles
but truthfully,
it could strip your body down
to the barest nutrients if you let it;
it could rebuild you bone by bone
and stone by stone.

There is loss in the world;
only a river can make it right.
When you uncover your wound
and give it to the river
like the belly of a resting gull,
like an alder leaf,
like any curling and fragile thing
that proves the water's surface is taut,
the river washes it bright and clean.

You have a choice then:
clasp your hand over the wound
or know, deeply,
that you are fertile and well-watered earth
worthy of planting seeds in.

iii. Why are you here?

There are mornings when the light
is heavy, and the weight of it
holds us to the ground. There is only
one direction then. One way
for the river to flow, the rain to fall:

down.

There are mornings when all things
lean toward the light, and the weight of it
gives us deep roots. You became the light
and you gifted us your multitude
of directionality.

You are glint, water, movement;
you are soil, taproot, stone.
You are living, most of all
in your leaving. You are the current
that carries medicine to us and through us
and you are the gleam
we stretch toward.

No river is a monument,
not even in the eager eyes
of gulls and ravens at the slow exhale
of spawning time.

But all rivers, in their way,
are monumental.

   iv. What are you for?

There are four things about you
that make my rib cage bloom
like wild aster trusting in the sun:

The quietness of your arrival
and the power of what you bring with you
in your hands like fir bark split
from the trunk.

(The others come later.)

I buried my face in the river,
breath held, eyes open.
When I stood upright, I learned
I could navigate by birdsong
and see love like landmarks.

I watched loss drift seaward;
the water makes it light.
I watched grief carried east;
it floats in the hush and chill.
But mostly, I was staggered
by the blessings that blossomed
in the morning air.

There are four things about you
that make my rib cage crack like stone
from the roots and the rainwater
of your love:

The quietness of your departure
and the power of what you leave behind.

(The others came before.)

You came before and, like all rivers,
you will constantly and softly
return.

September

We are in the time of radiant rot;
berries drop from the stems
when we shake them and salmon
eat up the daylight
as their flesh falls away from
their living bones.

We can feel the full weight
of our grief now
as everything that surrounds us
is shot through with final gold
and the world lays down its work
to rest.

The stillness is like a fresh layer
of humus on the ground.

We are hushed
as though we've entered a house
where someone is dying:
we hear nothing but the thuds of crab apples
falling into the yellowed grass.

Spring

Lift up your chin
and drop your shoulders
away from your ears.

Take one deep breath
for your ancestors,
one for yourself,
and one for the world yet to come.

It is permissible
to come to this work hesitant,
tired, wounded.

In spring even the bitterest greens
resolve toward eventual sweetness.

Take one breath for rest,
another for regeneration.

We don't criticize the tight buds
for asking that their needs be met
before they unfurl into leaves
and blooms.

Let tentative birdsong
become a clamour;
let leaves become broad
and skies expansive
as you stretch your weary back,
pull back your shoulders.

Let everything you need
collide into the crest
of your waiting chest
as you breathe.

Summer

Go out into the world.

Stand or sit or hold your body
like a precious thing;
hold as much of your body as you can
exchanging gentle touch with the ground.

When you look around yourself,
name all the ways you see thriving
mapped onto your surroundings.

Now, name all the ways
that you map the abundance
onto what's around you.

You are intrinsic to the good work
happening around you;
breathe in your belonging;
breathe out the question,

How can I build kinship
and community in this moment?

Fall

Lean into your aches
and bruises.

Breathe in the gentle decay
of what flourished in front of you;
ready yourself for the deeper work
that happens beneath the mulch,
beneath the soil.

We are building humus
and telling stories.

What surrounds you
that no longer serves you?
Let it go.

Let it break down
and reimagine itself.

Reimagine yourself too
and breathe into the ways
your body holds the work you do:

embody only what serves you.

Carry it in your bones.

Winter

Turn inward.

Is the tenacity of chlorophyll
held in your taut muscles?

Are ripeness and over-ripeness
at rest within you?

Is it time to settle in?

You are cycles;
you are systems.

The cold days may be lean
but there is a glut of stories in you.

Breathe in cool air.
Breathe out the first line of a story.

Inhale and exhale
until the right story surfaces;
let it take its time arriving.

Then keep yourself warm in its telling.

If your body is curling inward,
let it be like a seed and not a stone;
let it hold itself compact
without shedding its patient need
to unfurl someday
when the warmth and light
are promised to it again.

Húmá

Which is the most replenishing rain?

The one that soaks the roots of unseen flowers,
that gives conifer tips permission
to be so green in spring?

The one that teaches cedar
how to bind our hurts and cleanse us?

The one that melts away the lingering ice
and gives us sure footing in midwinter?

Which rain do we need the most?

The one that soaks the bog
and shows us where the topsoil is thin?

The one that sounds like a shell rattle
rapping against the rooftop?

The one that makes things cling to us
like pine sap, like joy, like wanting?

A Haíɫzaqv Taxonomy

Does it nourish?
Who is nourished in their body?
In their heart?

Does it heal?

Who is healed in their body?
In their spirit?

Does it equip?

Who builds and braids it?
Cuts, cradles, creates?

Does it teach?

Who does it edify?
Who builds systems from its stories?

If it does not nourish or heal,
equip or teach, what does it invite?

Who are its kin?
Do you know you are its kin?

Auricle and Miracle

Close your eyes.

Where in your body do you feel
a hummingbird's flight pattern?

For me it's the base of my skull,
radiating through my vertebrae
even before the sound trembles
against my eardrum.

The sound invites us to breathe out
the cramped isolation of winter,
to pull back our shoulders
like our rib cage is ready to bloom—
salmonberry blossoms, uncurling
fiddleheads, sturdy dandelions
and the pink bells of huckleberries.

Hummingbirds ask us
what is seeded inside us, waiting
for the light and warmth—
what parts of us embody spring,
movement, clarity.

These marvels are inside us,
patterned by tiny wings.

Dirt Prayer

What does it mean to feel grounded?

Imagine tender roots forming,
stretching their small hands outward
for nourishment.

How do the parts of you
that are in contact with the earth
form attachment to place?

What do you gain from this attachment?

Imagine blunt roots, grown roots,
reaching outward from your palms
as they meet this holy ground
(all ground is holy).

How is it you've become unshakeable?
Impervious to wind and weather?

It is borrowed strength, friend.

The soil is our mother;
hold your body against hers
when you need comfort.

The soil is our mother;
she unifies us in our communal need
to be held, to be strengthened by roots,

to be rooted in strength.

Crushed Wild Mint

How do you appease
a spirit?

Braid your hair, then
ask that spirit how it needs
to be loved.

If you are someone
who feeds the living,
ask yourself
how to nourish a ghost;

set three places
at the table
for the two of you
and for Grief.

Crush wild mint
and put it in your pockets,
in your hair,
in a bowl on the table.

Let the scent
cleanse Grief like smoke,
like cedar, like tenderness.

V

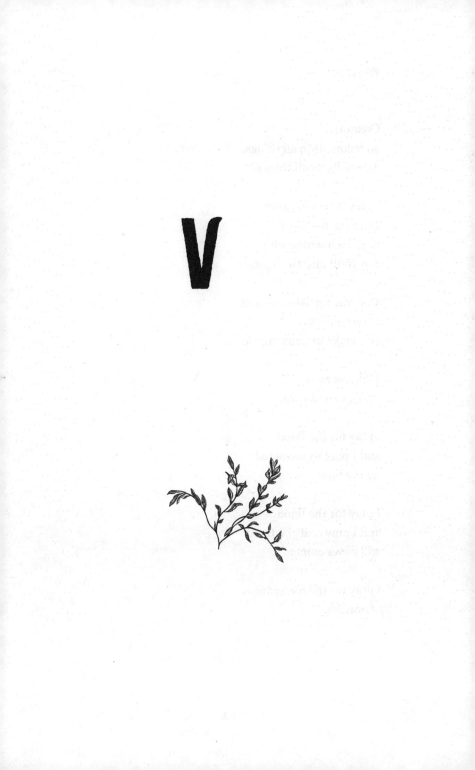

Prayer (I)

Creator,
go before us in all things,
especially small things.

Every inch you carve
from the darkness
is an inch where we
can swell into the light.

Take the terrible holiness
of our bodies
and make us consumable.

Make us each
into a sacred feast.

I pray for the flood
and I pray to be spared
by the flood.

I pray for the flood
and I pray that the flood
will never come;

I pray for the blessedness
of erasure.

Remembering the Flood

No one knows why the flood came.

Since Creation,
we had grown along the shoreline like dune grass
and nestled in the forest like wild blueberry bushes,
like salal; our feet were planted in the ground.

This is the rich earth we came from.

Then the waters began to rise.

. . .

There was no foretelling,
no agitation of birds, no time
to think of how I might uproot myself.
I looked down as water swept
around my ankles in bright, alarming
eddies.

I watched my brothers transform into eagles
and my sisters into sea wolves,
but me, my roots were buried too deep;
I had forgotten how to transform.

So many of us have forgotten how to transform.

. . .

I watched the flood waters rise
as I trimmed bulrushes and feather shafts
to extend my breath by inches.
The water was around my knees,
around my hips,
swallowing our holy ground
and everything that might someday become
holy ground.

Everything I loved was underwater,
and I, lonely and holy, felt it slip over my shoulders
like a heavy blanket of mountain goats' wool.

. . .

My bones will become a reef, I thought,
and in spite of my sadness I smiled a little.
Someday needlefish and rock crabs
will shelter in my rib cage. My scapulae
will be heavy with barnacles, with mussels.

. . .

Have you ever looked at the sky,
unflinching because you are incapable of flinching,
your neck arched and your chin tilted
and your ears deafened by salt water?
There is no sky more whole
than the sky that is perfectly above the line of your
    spine,
the sky that pins you to the earth.

I thought about what I might regret:
the ripe berries and fireweed blossoms
I'd never grind in my molars, the sphagnum
I'd never feel collapsing beneath the soles of my feet.

My knees and my hips ached
as the water rose and I willed my body to grow taller
so my head would be above the water a little longer,
my face to the sky.

. . .

The valley that swings from the ocean
to the ankles of M̓n̓sǧm̓x̌λi
is gone.

Clam beds no longer intertidal
but drowned.

Devil's club and wild currants,
licorice fern and rice root lily,
all salt dwellers now.

The water climbs patiently up the ridges.
The sky dims for me, the ocean exploring my face
with clumsy hands before continuing to crane upward.
I look down, and my heels have become stones.

    . . .

When I hear the thunderbird rumble
and feel the mountain quake, I think,
How did we miss the signs
of a multiplied disaster?
but as my lungs become pitchers
and the salt water sings into my mouth,
I feel the mountain's profound relief
radiate up into my granite heels.

    . . .

The mountain is animate.

The mountain has grown.

The mountain is not alone.

. . .

Before the moment when I feel nothing,
I feel gratitude:

the mountain is risen
and my loves with heels of flesh and bone
can rise a little higher too.

Ýúzua

Then Q̇ağm̓i asked,
"Are you still above water?"

"No," said Ṁṇsğm̓x̌λi,
"I am about to be drowned."

Then Q̇ağm̓i took a mass of rock
and threw it at Ṁṇsğm̓x̌λi
in order to make Ṁṇsğm̓x̌λi higher.

i.

This is our flood story, brother:
you make my sorrow
into ceremony.

Gift me something of your body
when the water is rocking
against my bruised heels:
enough so that I rise
a little higher.

Gift me something of your body
when the water wears my uneven ankles smooth
like they are soft limestone,
like time is a circle.

Be a mountain
that has manifested, briefly,
as a man.

ii.

This is our flood story, brother:
you make my loss
into ceremony.

Give me the boldness of your shoulder
and a clamshell full of blood
when the water rises over my heart
and I face east, cedar boughs in my hands.

Gift me one of your bones,
something small, or a curving rib
with stories in the marrow
and a surface like basalt.

Be a man
who has manifested, briefly,
as a mountain.

iii.

This is our flood story, brother:
you make my grief
into ceremony.

Gift me the height gained
by a deep breath and a straight back,
the height of a well spirit
whose momentary body
is striving toward the rattles and whistles
of our ancestors.

Gift me the strength
of your back muscles,
the tender discipline of the braid
that rests in alignment with your spine,
as the water circles my neck
like a cedar-bark ring
and I hear the sound of a thunderbird's wings.

     iv.

This is our flood story, brother:
you make my living
into ceremony.

When the flood rises past my jaw
and I can only speak to you through water,
manifest as a mountain and raise me up higher
with your granite
and your good earth
and your patience that is more resilient
than any alpine bloom.

You are taller than me, brother,
your chin resting like a cloud
on the high meadow of my hair,
your hands on my arms as heavy as the colour
of a hawk against the sky.

v.

This is our flood story, brother:
you make my love
into ceremony.

My children's children
will rub their little fingers along
the parts of you that you gifted to me
when the waters rose,
the height you gave me
until the waters receded
and I could take a deep breath in;

they will map the parts of me
that were parts of you in the time before.

Your grandchildren's grandchildren
will rub their little fingers
along the parts of me that I gifted to you
when the rising waters brought you low
and I learned how to be a mountain
so I could lift you up too.

    vi.

This is our story, brother:
we are mountains
that help other mountains
withstand the flood.

Mountains Teach Us (I)

Stories require witnesses
and the witnesses are not always
human kin.

You can climb to the crown
of Q̓aǧm̓i's head, and you should,
and when you do
you and the false azalea
and the tidal waves of songbirds
will be the witnesses
this story requires:

There are spaces on Q̓aǧm̓i's head
where a loving hand
has lifted part of him away.

You can climb to the crown
of M̓n̓sǧm̓x̌λi's head, and you should,
and when you do
you and the scrub cedar
and the careless grouse and sure-footed deer
will be the witnesses
this story requires:

There is stone on the scalp of M̓n̓sǧm̓x̌λi
not of that body,
resting atop that mountain
like a cedar hat.

This is the kind of love
that makes my body
shatter into inlets;

this is the kind of story
that puts a mineral glitter
on the world.

Mountains teach us reciprocity.

Instructions for Climbing Ṃ̓ṇsg̓ṃx̌λi

i. You have no idea, no idea

You have no idea
how long the valley is.

Long valleys leave you time
to imagine many summits
while you're still at sea level.
You can walk for hours,
first delicately parting the salal,
then, when your muscles begin to ache,
falling indelicately through the underbrush.
You can walk for hours,
and still you won't gain any height.

Don't despair, love.
Long valleys leave you time
to imagine many summits
so your spirit can climb
a thousand mountains
while your body climbs
the singular mountain
in front of you.

Let your spirit ache
with a thousand climbs.

ii. Eventual ascents

When the mountain is ready for you,
you'll start to ascend.

You might have the instinct
(it'll be wrong) to follow the rivers;
you might think rivers are the backbones
of a watershed

and that a watershed
will introduce you to a mountain.

The truth is that watersheds
are multitudes, and that the ridges
which demarcate the tender valleys
are the spines you really want to follow.

Water chooses the steepest way,
but ridges will sway you upward
if you ask them,
and bridge you from the ocean
to the sky.

iii. Don't be alarmed

If you're halfway up the mountain
and the surprising heat of spring sun
breaks through,
delicately peel away your clothes
like the outer layer of a salmonberry shoot
and use your whole body
to feel out a breeze.

Don't be alarmed:
neither the grouse
nor the songbirds
can laugh in any language
we understand,

and the blackflies will be grateful.

iv. You have arrived

Did you know that some mountains
have changeable summits,
peaks that do not always rest
in the same space?

These are living
geographies.

This is especially true
when the crown of a mountain
was a gift from the weary body
of that mountain's brother.

You will arrive at the summit
when you feel you can't climb any higher;
you'll be at the top
when you're most deeply tired.

This is mountain magic:
it isn't measured in elevation
but in the widest possible valley
between your exhaustion
and your elation.

The joy is coming.

Instructions for Climbing Q̇ağṃi

i. Your favourite ancestor is your starting point

Across the inlet
is my ancestor.

Cemeteries are impersonal,
but this is not a cemetery;
it is a burial. Moss and bone.

I part the low-swung cedar at sea level
and before I even begin
to feel the climb in my joints,
I am beside his skull
at the foot of a small cliff.

(I hope someday
to have a cliff for a headstone.)

The bone of his skull is brown
as though it soaked in the tannins
that make our coastal hues rich.

We do not move bones here
so I'm relieved at the orientation
of his skull:

it's important that he faces the inlet,
can see Q̇ağṃi through his cedar veil.

Sometimes I go to him
to keep company,
and we look out at the mountain together.
Sometimes we talk.

And this is how I remember where the journey begins:

I go to my favourite ancestor
and follow his gaze.

I don't know if he ever climbed Q̇aǧm̱i
but he was a tall man,
more like a mountain
than a man who climbs mountains.

Still, the land both is and contains
the bones of our ancestors
and whether or not he climbed it
he is my guide.

To climb a mountain,
find your favourite ancestor
and follow their gaze
like a trail.

ii. Look for the gifts from the mountain

I will tell you this now
and you'll know it in your bones
when you come down from your mountain.

You think the medicine will be at the top,
that you have to earn it with the climb.

You're wrong.

Soon you'll realize the medicine
is all tumbling seaward,
thanks to gravity and love;

the mountain is tender
and wants us to be well.

iii. The medicine shows the way

When I started my journey
I saw ḣáúx̌vsúlí at sea level.

There were no trails
except deer trails that melted
into mountain goat trails,
and as I gained elevation
I watched for ḣáúx̌vsúlí
to show me the way.

This is the right way,
I thought to myself, comforted
whenever I saw the deeply ribbed leaves
spiralling around those heavy stalks,
imagining the dense chaos
of the roots plunging deep in the soil.

Let me be so rooted.

Follow the medicine, I thought;
the medicine knows the right way.

But listen carefully:

at the end of my journey
the ḣáúx̌vsúlí whispered,

I wasn't telling you that you were right.

I was telling you that you were safe.

iv. Improbable flowers (transitions)

You will know that you're on
the cusp of transfiguration
when you see flowers you don't recognize:

Pink mountain-heather
and unexpected asters,
marsh marigold and eventually,
wild lupines.

This is not sea-level botany.

This is the mountain speaking
in flowers.

You're gaining elevation, my darling.
Look for your bouquet.

v. Snow in July

The best time to climb a mountain
is during a time of transition.

Transition for you or for the mountain.

I like to climb in the summer
so the heat makes me feel

a little delirious, like I'm taking in the world
with no barriers—my vision
disconcertingly clear, the roar of horseflies
overwhelming.

When you reach a good height,
even in July, the freckles of snow
you saw from sea level
start to yawn in front of you.

You will eat snow with the joy of a small child
who has never seen snow before,
skim the debris of winter and spring
off the surface to reach the granular drift beneath,
sweeping whole seasons aside
with your raw and powerful fingertips.

Nothing in your life will ever feel better
than massaging that chilly offering into the hair
at the back of your neck, roughly washing your face
with both your hands full of gritty snow.
You will shudder from the base of your spine
when the high breezes touch your damp skin
and it will be good.

    vi. Follow the blackfly whine

You are close.
Do you know how close you are?

The blackflies know.

They'll swarm you upward
if you let them.

They will bring you
from the treeline to the summit
with a gentleness
you will strive to emulate all your life.

Let us love you, they'll sing.

vii. Hawks from above

Seeing a red-tailed hawk,
in flight, from above:

You can stand at the edge
of a bluff, looking down,
and finally understand the name.

Sunlight through bull kelp ribbons,
red ochre pictographs,
the inner bark of spring alder—
when you reach the summit
and see a hawk from above,
colours become truer.

This is what summits gift us.
You cannot see this shade from below.

If you're feeling brave,
ask the hawk for a feather.
You'll find it amidst the lichen
and warm, exposed stones,
the low, slow cedar
and the partridgefoot blossoms
that look like stubborn blots of snow.

When you hold that feather later,
delicately, between your thumb
and your forefinger,
remember how it felt
to see a hawk's bright tail from above
when you stood at the peak of the world.

viii. Life below sunset

You've seen a sunset before,
the sun sweeping in a lazy arc,
pulling a rippling tail of wild colours
down to the horizon and below it.

But sunsets at summits
are strange little birds:
their tails fan out in all directions.

Lay back in the damp moss
and trickles of starflowers;
no matter how you tilt your chin
the sunset will be vivid
and all around you.

ix. And sunrise too

Wait. Take a slow breath in,
and let it out while imagining petals
falling from your lips.

Breath and air at the summit
have an unaccustomed lightness.

The sunrise, too, will envelop you and the sky
like the flush of colour that returns to your body
as you emerge from an alpine lake
and shake water droplets like crystals
from your hair.

First paleness, like a bunchberry bloom—
then the firm pink of a healthy nail bed—
then gentle riots of red
that put huckleberries and sockeye flesh to shame.

You are below the sunrise
and beside it
and within it
and it holds you,
it holds you.

Mountains hold you.
The sky holds you.

x. You'll forget the descent

Time has a spine
that is not straight
when you stand at the summit
of a mountain.

But you cannot stay there.

Sea level needs you.

You'll forget the descent,
the way gravity tumbles you down
and makes your thighs burn.

You'll cut into the soft flesh
between your thumb and index finger
as copperbush and small cedars
run through them,
slowing your momentum on the slopes.

The heels of your hands
will be indented by the rocks you use
to lower yourself into creek beds.

You'll forget the descent
and wonder where your bruises came from,
the taste of wild blueberries lingering
between your teeth.

The contour lines and medicine lines
will guide you down
even if your eyes are closed;
trust the mountain.

You'll forget the descent
but never the gifts:
quartz crystals in your pockets
and hemlock needles
that rain from your hair.

xi. Sea level

Do you remember how to exist
at sea level?

This is where you are a true iteration of yourself—
a quick and fragile little creature
built for liminal spaces and transitions
between shore and forest.

But you become truer
when the mountain lowers you down
to sea level again.

Let your shoulders sink
with the sweet relief of a receding tide.
Put your hand on your sternum
and as you breathe, remember the firmness
of boulders beneath your palms.
Remember how the mountain breathes
through its days of wild lupine
and its nights of mosquito song.

Do you remember how to exist
at sea level?

The last word the mountain gives you,
if you listen, is a benediction.

Love Poem

Stand still:

I can slide my fingertip
over your weary skin
in the shape of the inlets
below us.

Like any Haíłzaqv woman
when I smell hemlock
I taste salt and imagine the taut snap
of herring eggs bursting
between my teeth.

When I taste salt
I remember the sweat
of your body,
the heat of your body,
your edible exhaustion.

Ask yourself, honestly:
What if you're holy?

Alpine love
is mutual witnessing
and you are the author
of the prayers that I pray.

Hṇ́qvṇ́x̌

Can you imagine
what the world looked like
in the time of the flood?

The shorelines we know so intimately,
the slow swell of islands,
the low valleys and hills—
hidden away like the rattles and aprons
and button blankets
we settle into cedar chests
during our times of grief.

Can you imagine
what the world looked like
without geography?

I can imagine:

Stand at the summit of Q̇ağṃi
or even at the summit of Ṃṇsğṃx̌λi
when the fog settles in.

The world is erased
and all that exists is the ground
under your feet,
the ground under the feet of your brother
or your sister if they're standing
on that other mountain in the distance.

The fog reminds us
of how small the world was
for our ancestors
who could not transform—
of the gratitude we owe mountains
for lifting our people up,
putting hands on their shoulders
and standing brow to brow
with the mothers who would birth mothers
who would someday birth us.

We owe such a debt
to the tenderness of mountains
and to the fog that teaches us
to remember.

Mountains Teach Us (II)

When I climbed to the crown
of M̓n̓sǧm̓x̌λi,
I found a little truth
that had been waiting for me
in the marrow of my bones:

It was time for M̓n̓sǧm̓x̌λi
to gift something back
to his brother.

. . .

When I climbed to the crown
of Q̓aǧm̓i,
I laid some stones carried
from one summit to another
and I found another little truth:

The mutual care of mountains
grinds time like glaciers
and leaves unexpected marks
and obligations on us all.

So I carried some stones
from Q̓aǧm̓i
to gift back to M̓n̓sǧm̓x̌λi again.

. . .

The gift economies of mountains
make us into bridges between peaks,
bridges that stretch over islands and inlets
across the backs of thousands of gulls.

. . .

Mountains teach us kinship.

Mountains teach us generosity.

Prayer (II)

Creator,
go before us in all things,
especially small things.

Every inch of light
you gift us teaches us
how to decay the shadows.

Every inch of water
you gift us teaches us
how to float without drifting.

The flood has come
and we have survived the flood.

The flood may come again
and we will survive it again.

I pray for the blessedness
of perpetual memory.

ACKNOWLEDGEMENTS

Ǧiáxsix̌a to Dan for keeping me fed on good wild meat and for keeping the garden growing. Noen and Magnus, my sweetest ones, thank you for all the joy you give me. To my ḥbúkv, thank you for loving me unconditionally. And Gwani, I'll always be grateful for the peace of rewriting poems while you napped beside me in the sunshine; I miss you every day.

Ǧiáxsix̌a to Haydn, Dia, Chris and Cayce for being my most patient readers, and to Ric Young and the incomparably beautiful Louise Dennys for the guidance and love that only the wisest of godparents could proffer. Ǧiáxsix̌a to Christopher for nourishing me with lingcod livers and to Jerry, my Dutch uncle, for being the first one to believe I was a poet.

GLOSSARY

*All words listed are from Heiltsuk
unless otherwise identified.*

ǧáǧm̓ · grandmother

ǧiáxsix̌a · thank you

Gwani · Granny

Haíłzaqv · Heiltsuk

ḣáúx̌vsúlí · false hellebore

ḣbúkv · mother

ḣl̓xvbís · blood

ḣn̓q̓vn̓x̌ · foggy season

húmá · to ask

luáł · ghost

máłuala · two people walking together

M̓n̓sǧm̓x̌λi · Mount Merritt

Q̓aǧm̓i · Mount Keyes

skuusiid (Haida) · an endemic variety of potato

wá · river

Wúgvmi · Creator

x̌ásákv · ocean

ýúzua · flood

ABOUT THE AUTHOR

Jess Housty ('Cúagilákv) is a parent, writer and grass-roots activist with Heiltsuk and mixed settler ancestry. They serve their community as an herbalist and land-based educator alongside broader work in the non-profit and philanthropic sectors. They are inspired and guided by relationships with their homelands, their extended family and their non-human kin, and they are committed to raising their children in a similar framework of kinship and land love. They reside and thrive in their unceded ancestral territory in the community of Bella Bella, BC.